Welberg Vinicius Gomes Bonifácio

School subjects, interdisciplinarity and race relations

Welberg Vinicius Gomes Bonifácio

School subjects, interdisciplinarity and race relations

Towards a school education that contributes to anti-racism

ScienciaScripts

Imprint
Any brand names and product names mentioned in this book are subject to trademark, brand or patent protection and are trademarks or registered trademarks of their respective holders. The use of brand names, product names, common names, trade names, product descriptions etc. even without a particular marking in this work is in no way to be construed to mean that such names may be regarded as unrestricted in respect of trademark and brand protection legislation and could thus be used by anyone.

Cover image: www.ingimage.com

This book is a translation from the original published under ISBN 978-620-2-40501-0.

Publisher:
Sciencia Scripts
is a trademark of
Dodo Books Indian Ocean Ltd. and OmniScriptum S.R.L publishing group

120 High Road, East Finchley, London, N2 9ED, United Kingdom
Str. Armeneasca 28/1, office 1, Chisinau MD-2012, Republic of Moldova, Europe
Printed at: see last page
ISBN: 978-620-8-31288-6

SUMMARY

INTRODUCTION

A society free of racism and racial inequalities is still a challenge to be overcome and school education can and must contribute to developing this process. Law 10.639/03, which made the teaching of Afro-Brazilian history and culture compulsory in basic education, is a milestone in the construction of education for race relations[1] and anti-racism in schools. This law is the basis for the development of educational policies, especially with regard to the reorganization of curricula and teaching materials in basic education schools and teacher training. However, much still needs to be done to ensure that Law 10.639/03 is applied effectively, so that as a result we have an education that contributes to overcoming racism.

One of the main obstacles to the realization of pedagogical practices that address racial relations in education in a positive and formative way is related to teacher training, which does not adequately prepare teachers to deal with these issues within schools. Although teachers recognize the importance of this issue for education, they don't know how to approach it or have difficulties doing so.

This book consists of study material aimed at training teachers in the perspective of education for racial relations and aims to help them rethink their pedagogical practices, as well as mitigate the difficulties in working with racial issues in the school environment. In this way, it enables teachers to develop a view of racial issues within the subjects they teach in schools and the possible connections with other school knowledge.

To begin with, we present a general overview of teacher training policies

---

[1] We have chosen to use the term "raga" rather than "ethnicity" because we understand it as a sociological concept that is crucial to understanding the issues that concern black people in Brazil, especially prejudice, discrimination and exclusion related to being black. Although many of our references make use of the concept "ethno-racial", which is the most commonly found in academic productions and can cover indigenous blacks, gypsies and descendants of other migrant groups, in our speeches we replace this concept with the term "racial", taking into account the specificities surrounding the history and lives of black people in Brazil, marked above all by the context of racism. For further information on this issue, we suggest reading the text "How to work with 'raga' in sociology" by Antonio Sergio Alfredo Guimaraes, published by Revista Educagao e Pesquisa, Sao Paulo, v.29, n.1, p. 93-107, Jan./Jun. 2003.

focused on racial issues, highlighting the importance of including this topic in initial teacher training, regardless of the specific area of training, in order to prepare teachers for a pedagogical practice that contributes to valuing black history and culture and combating racism. We therefore discuss some of the legal frameworks such as Resolution 01/2004 and Opinion 03/2004 of the CNE - National Education Council, which set out objectives and guidelines for teacher training in relation to education for racial relations.

We then develop a discussion that results from a review of academic and intellectual productions such as books, doctoral theses, master's dissertations and scientific articles, which deal with the theme of race, especially black history and culture in various areas of science and school subjects in basic education. Thus, seeking a productive meaning both for the development of the work, as well as for possible readers, this study material corresponds to syntheses of reflections that permeate the intentionality of these writings, which is to present possibilities for a pedagogical practice focused on education for racial relations in order to involve all teachers and all school subjects.

The theoretical basis presented here can help schools to develop activities that can address a variety of themes that deal with racial issues, including: Characters from Brazilian history: "heroes from all over the world - TV Cultura"; Black and black literature in Brazilian literature; Racism and discriminatory practices in society (racial segregation); Black feminism (Lelia Gonzales, Bell Hooks, etc.); Portrayals of black people in the Brazilian media (Lelia Gonzales, Bell Hooks, etc.).); Portrayals of black people in the Brazilian media (Documentary "A negagao do Brasil"); Music and the racial question (samba, rap, kuduro, etc.); Capoeira, cultural tradition and black resistance in Brazil; Afro-Brazilian religiosity (Candomble, umbanda, tambor de mina, congado, etc.); The historical division of slavery in Brazil.); The historical division of slavery: the need for affirmative public policies for the black population in Brazil; The insertion of black people in Brazilian society and racial inequalities in Brazil (work, income, education, etc.); The black phenotype: skin color and hair as racial markers; Africa, technological development and scientific production (deconstructing the stereotype of backwardness); African games and logical-mathematical reasoning. These themes are only suggestions, and it is up to the teachers to address other issues related to racial issues that can be linked to the curriculum content and that are of interest to them and their students.

In this way, we present indications so that it is possible to think and/or rethink pedagogical practices, in order to seek a direction that is geared towards an education for racial relations, anti-racism and the valorization of black history and culture, and the adoption of an interdisciplinary stance in its approaches.

In this way, the proposal aims to create the conditions for teachers to be able to establish relationships between school subjects and the issue of race, with the aim of valuing and stimulating protagonism, respecting teacher autonomy in the construction of knowledge and school practices in the most appropriate way for the school context in which they are inserted.

1 - TEACHER TRAINING POLICIES AND EDUCATION FOR RACIAL RELATIONS

The enactment of Law 10.639/03 has given direction to the elaboration, development and application of public policies aimed at realizing the constitutional principle of equality, especially with regard to the logic of racial equality. Thus, we see the development of federal, state and municipal projects, mainly linked to educational bodies, which aim to provide training for teachers that meets the objectives of this law.

However, a major problem is that most of this training takes place in continuing education, extension and postgraduate courses, and does not effectively reach the majority of teachers. It is important that the issue is addressed in initial training in undergraduate courses, so that students become teachers able to work with this issue when they finish their degrees, thus making the application of current legislation and the search for the construction of racial equality in our country more effective.

Law 10 639/03 came about as a response to a historic social demand for policies that contribute to the construction of racial equality. In this sense, Santos (2011) states that:

> The Law repositions black people and race relations in education - transforming what is silenced (such as racism in everyday school life) into a denunciation and problematization, drawing attention to how apparently "neutral" knowledge contributes to the reproduction of racial stereotypes and stigmas and to racism. Law 10639 sets us the challenge of building an education for racial equality, a human formation that promotes non-racist values (p.5).

However, even more than a decade after its promulgation, its effects on society, and especially on education, still appear timidly or inefficiently, given the lack of universalization of educational policies that help consolidate the application of this Law. In this respect, Santos also states that:

> [...] there is no law whose application is automatically defined. Every application of the law is the result of disputes between interpretations. This allows, at the same time, for the application of Law 10.639 to take up aspects inherent in the broad educational agenda of the Black Movement or, on the other hand, for it to be simplified, reproducing educational processes that do

> not fulfill the function of combating values that sustain racism. The main enforcers of 10.639 are the members of the school community (as well as the agents of educational policy production), who then become interlocutors of the Brazilian Black Movement from the moment it positions itself as a social actor that disputes and intervenes in the construction of education (2011, p.06).

These points show us that we need to rethink various aspects of teacher training, given that the issue of race is neglected in most undergraduate courses, so many of our teachers leave their degrees without the minimum preparation needed to deal with the issue in the school environment, which is, according to Santos (p.7 2011) "made up mostly of actors who have not been prepared to constitute an anti-racist education". In this way, it doesn't make it possible to develop relevant work with a critical approach that actually contributes to overcoming racism and seeking racial equality, or simply corroborates the fact that part of the school community doesn't care about these discussions, because they don't understand their social implications, either in the school environment or outside of it.

> In general, the literature on education and ethnic-racial relations points out that teachers are unprepared and/or insecure to deal with situations related to students' racial belonging (SILVA, 2009, p.18).

This highlights the importance of evaluating the need to include subjects dealing with race relations in the official curricula of degree courses, with a view to training teachers to work in the classroom with themes linked to Law No. 10 639/03. This law makes it compulsory to study "Afro-Brazilian History and Culture" in the official school curriculum.

This issue can contribute to the dissemination and production of knowledge and to building teachers' critical awareness of racial plurality, making them capable of acting competently, helping to guarantee respect for legal rights for all, with a view to fully consolidating Brazilian democracy.

In this way, training teachers who take into account the teaching process, the recognition and valorization of identity, history and culture of black origin, as well as guaranteeing recognition, equality and valorization of African roots and overcoming racism.

> the Law is a regulator of the construction of the curriculum, it is also a

> curriculum, but it is a "prescription" - and it is not necessarily applied, or its application is mediated by the interpretations of the actors involved. The existence of the law does not guarantee anti-racist education. This is a construction in the field of concrete curricular "practices" (SANTOS, 2011, p.8).

From the north to the south of Brazil, public bodies and educational institutions (especially higher education institutions) are debating public policies to promote racial equality, with a view to establishing a democratic state of rights, offering all citizens equal access to education (including higher education), health and social justice, among other aspects. Knowing that *Brazil's racial democracy* is a widespread myth in the national imagination, we need to be aware that the marks left by three centuries of slavery in Brazil still need to be truly remedied, as well as the social shortcomings and the burden of prejudice and discrimination that began during this period and which continue to this day.

Another important milestone was the publication of the National Education Council's resolution, Resolugao CNE/CP n° 1, of June 17, 2004 (DOU n° 118, 22/6/2004, Segao 1, p. 11). 11), which establishes the National Curricular Guidelines for the Education of Ethnic-Racial Relations and for the Teaching of Afro-Brazilian and African History and Culture, to be practiced by institutions at all levels of education, especially by institutions that develop initial and continuing teacher training programs. This document prescribes that "Higher Education Institutions shall include in the content of subjects and curricular activities of the courses they teach, Ethnic-Racial Relations Education, as well as the treatment of issues and themes that concern Afro-descendants" (CNE /CP Resolution No. 1, of June 17, 2004, p.01).

This resolution also places responsibility on the federative entities to ensure that these guidelines are put into practice, establishing that: "It will be up to the Education Councils of the States, the Federal District and the Municipalities to develop the National Curriculum Guidelines established by this Resolution, within the framework of collaboration and the autonomy of the federative entities and their respective systems" (CNE /CP Resolution No. 1, of June 17, 2004, p.01).

CNE/CP Resolution No. 1, of June 17, 2004, was instituted in accordance with the opinion of the National Education Council, CNE/CP Opinion No. 3, of March 10, 2004.° 3, of March 10, 2004, taking into account, with regard to the training of teachers, the requirement that higher education institutions should include in the content of subjects and curricular activities of the courses they teach the education of racial relations, as well as the treatment of issues and themes concerning Afro-Brazilians, where it is necessary to:

> Inclusion of discussion of the racial issue as an integral part of the curriculum matrix, both in degree courses for Early Childhood Education, the initial and final years of Primary Education, Media Education, Youth and Adult Education, and in continuing teacher training processes, including teachers in higher education (Parecer CNE/CP n.° 3, de 10 de margo de 2004, p.14).

The result of these initiatives is training that enables teachers to understand the importance of racial issues in society, especially in schools. But also so that they are prepared to deal positively with these issues, mobilizing knowledge and resources to develop pedagogical strategies that can contribute to an education for racial relations and anti-racism, so that Brazil can provide all people with a formal education taught by teachers who are prepared "to deal with the tense relationships produced by racism and discrimination, who are sensitive to and capable of leading the re-education of relationships between different ethno-racial groups, i.e. between descendants of Africans, Europeans, Asians and indigenous peoples" (Parecer CNE/CP n.° 3, of March 10, 2004, p.02).

In this way, the aim is to consolidate a teaching staff in basic education that is "capable of positively directing relations between people of different ethnic-racial backgrounds, in the sense of respect and the correction of prejudiced postures, attitudes and words" (Parecer CNE/CP n.° 3, de 10 de margo de 2004, p.08).

In this sense, racial relations education aims to disseminate and produce knowledge, as well as attitudes, attitudes and values that educate citizens about racial plurality, making them capable of interacting and negotiating common objectives that guarantee respect for legal rights and the valorization of identity, in the quest to consolidate Brazilian democracy.

In order to achieve this, this opinion makes it clear what the responsibilities of institutions, education systems and their members are within this process, emphasizing that:

> On the basis of this opinion, it will be up to the education systems, the schools, the pedagogical coordination of the educational establishments and the teachers to establish teaching content, units of study, projects and programs, covering the different curricular components. It will be up to the administrators of the education systems and providers to provide the schools, their teachers and students with bibliographical and other teaching materials, as well as monitoring the work carried out, in order to prevent such complex issues, which are very little dealt with in both initial and continuing teacher training, from being addressed in a summarized, incomplete and flawed manner (Parecer CNE/CP n.° 3, de 10 de margo de 2004, p.08-09).

Based on these discussions, this book aims to help ensure that education on race relations can be effective in Brazilian basic education schools, through the pedagogical practice of the teachers who are part of them.

2 - THE SUBJECTS CONSIDERED PRIORITIES FOR THE WORKING WITH RACE EDUCATION

The subjects of History, Art Education and Literature appear in the body of Law 10.639/03 as priority areas for working with racial themes.

It is in this sense that we seek to address the possible contributions of this school knowledge to an education for racial relations.

2.1 - African and Afro-Brazilian history and race relations in the world history teaching

To begin our discussion of history teaching and race relations in education, we will present some of Oliva's (2003) questions, which serve as a starting point for the reflections presented here, where the author poses the following questions:

> How many of us studied Africa when we were in school? How many had the subject History of Africa in their history courses? How many books or texts have we read on the subject? Apart from the brief incursions into National Geographic or Discovery Channel programs, or the shocking images of an African world in agony, of AIDS spreading, of hunger crushing, of ethnic groups clashing with great violence or of safaris and exotic animals, what do we know about Africa? (p.423).

In order to deal with the specific nature of the issue, it is necessary to take a look at the teaching of history, which can make a significant contribution to understanding the problem in question. One of the major questions asked by primary school students is why they study history. It seems to us that the way this subject is treated in the classroom often does not contribute much to establishing links between the content studied and the students' day-to-day experiences.

The teaching of history needs to enable students to think historically, breaking with the old response that we commonly hear from our teachers that studying history helps us learn about the past, think about the present and plan for the future. This answer seems true to us, but not convincing enough to make sense of the content being studied.

In this way, we understand that studying history consists of seeking to understand historical processes, the ways in which human actions have happened and are happening over time, both in terms of material and symbolic structures and in terms of the individual and collective dimensions.

In this sense, it's important to think about the intentionality of pedagogical practice in history teaching, so that we can look for possibilities to develop a critical capacity to interpret historical facts and current realities based on their historicity. In this way, the study of history enables students to perceive the reality in which they live, as well as their identity.

Oliva (2003) also contributes to these points by developing his interpretations of the teaching of African History, where he reports that:

> The job of historian or teacher - I can't see them being so separate - enables us to understand and analyze humanity in its journey through time. This can't happen just out of adoration for research or the power to tell stories. Going back to the past purely out of erudition or curiosity is not our task. The past communicates the present, the present dialogues with the past. Only in this way can our arduous task be filled with meaning and sense. I suspect that students think so too. If the History of Africa, as a field of human thought, justifies itself, in our case, the responsibility acquires a double weight (p.423).

When we discuss the teaching of history, we can't help but talk about historiography, in other words, the unfolding of historical narratives, given that, just as there is no scientific neutrality, the historiography that develops will be loaded with intentionality and subjectivity, a proper look on the part of those who tell the story. Often, the paths taken by historical narratives are linked to the interests of the groups in power. On this subject, Felipe & Teruya (2010), when discussing the History of Africa, report that "all the constructions elaborated about Africa have never distanced themselves from the ambiguity of dominating it and configuring it as a counterpoint to a Europe that arrogated to itself a dominant role" (p.06). This reinforces the understanding that there is no absolute truth or totality of events when it comes to historiography, which corresponds to a composition linked to a historical period, a culture and the conceptions of those who narrate. As Jenkins (2005, p.31) points out, "no historian can encompass and thus recover the totality of past events, because the content of these events is practically unlimited".

The history of a people can be told in different ways and what determines how it will be told is the method adopted by the historian, in other words, the paradigms that guide his perceptions and interpretations when looking at the object of investigation. In this sense, Jenkins (2005) also points out that history "is always bound to be a personal construction, a manifestation of the historian's perspective as a narrator" (p.33).

Thus, the inclusion of a new perspective on the history of Africa in historiographical production can present a dynamic that is not Eurocentric, because according to Santos (2012):

> This movement is expressed by the interest in studying and understanding other temporalities as well as the plurality of socio-cultural experiences, multiplying the objects, approaches and research problems taken on by historians (p.61).

These points give us a basis for beginning to understand why themes linked to the unfolding of African and Afro-Brazilian historical processes have been neglected, or worked on from prejudiced perspectives throughout the development of the history of education and history teaching in Brazil. These problems still need to be resolved, because as Felipe & Teruya (2010, p.01) state, "the history of Brazil without knowledge of African history is a unilateral white history, marked by Eurocentric conceptions".

Also contributing to these positions, Fernandes (2005) states that, "a more accurate analysis of the history of educational institutions in our country, through the curricula, teaching programs and textbooks shows a preponderance of the so-called 'superior and civilized' culture, of European origin" (p.379380). The contents referring to the History of Africa began to acquire greater visibility and notoriety in the last three decades, but it is still incipient. In this sense, Fernandes also denounces that:

> Despite the theoretical and methodological renewal of History in recent years, the syllabus for this subject in primary school has been based on a monocultural and Eurocentric view of our past. The study of the so-called "History of Brazil" begins with the arrival of the Portuguese, ignoring the indigenous presence prior to the process of conquest and colonization. The

> role of the Portuguese colonizer is extolled as the pathfinder and the only person responsible for the occupation of our territory. However, the genocide and ethnocide practiced against Brazil's indigenous populations is hidden: there were around 5 million at the time of the so-called "discovery", today there are no more than 350,000 Indians (2005, p.380).

In this context, the History of Africa is presented in a pejorative way, in order to exalt the supposed inferiority and evolutionary backwardness of African peoples and societies, because as Felipe & Teruya (2010, p.03) state, "the European imagination has devoted to African lands and their inhabitants a wide range of disqualifying injunctions, often supported by European intellectuals. Africa was condemned to the role of peripheral space of humanity".

The impact of this stance on history teaching tends to be reflected in the academic performance of those individuals who are not included in the teaching-learning process through the exclusion of their identities in the curricula, textbooks and teaching practices. Lima (2004) points out that "the misrepresented inclusion or deliberate exclusion of some aspects of this history can lead to the creation of an identity or self-image that is distinct from the reality of that human group, distorted or defined according to ideological elements that are far from the real world" (p.160). In this way, when students don't identify and recognize themselves in the school environment, they find it more difficult to make sense of the history content they are taught. It is no coincidence that black children and adolescents have higher dropout and failure rates in Brazil[2] . Fernandes (2005) also corroborates this interpretation when he states that:

> Curricula and textbooks that silence and even omit the condition of black and Amerindian populations as historical subjects have contributed to increasing the dropout and repetition rates of children from the poorest social strata. The vast majority enter school and leave early without completing their studies in elementary school because they don't identify with a school that is still modeled on Eurocentric standards, which doesn't value the ethno-cultural diversity of our education (p.380-381).

Based on the above, we can reflect on which History of Africa, written from which historiographical perspectives, should be taught in Brazilian schools so that we

---

[2] See "LOUZANO, Paula. School failure: evolution of educational opportunities for students from different racial groups. **Cadernos Cenpec**, Nova serie, v. 3, n. 1, 2013."

can contribute to achieving what black movements in Brazil have been fighting for for more than half a century, which is the end of racism and racial equality. Felipe & Teruya (2010) suggest that:

> African history should cover the dynamics of African societies in political, cultural and social terms, with an emphasis on the period from the 12th to the 18th century, because of its more direct impact on Brazilian society. Emphasizing the totality of the continent, of an experience common to all Africans, is justified because the separation into disconnected parts of the African continent has served the various manipulations of racist ideas about these peoples (p.02).

Analysing and understanding the history of the African continent and its peoples from this new perspective is essential for the school's educational process in exercising respect for diversity and consolidating an awareness of social justice, because "understanding and contextualizing information about aspects of the African continent is undoubtedly a critical exercise" (FELIPE & TERUYA, 2010, p.03).

One of the main factors justifying the teaching of black history and culture is related to the importance of this content for a better understanding of the historical processes and socio-cultural characteristics of Brazil on the part of the various racial groups that live here, "for reasons of the history of humanity or even the economic history of capitalism, a knowledge of African history would be indispensable" (FELIPE & TERUYA, 2010, p.06). This statement further highlights the importance of the theme here for the education of Brazilian students. The authors bring us other relevant arguments that help us understand the importance of African History content, pointing out that a:

> Africa had technologies, cultures and political organizations as advanced as those of the Europeans. This history allows for the construction of new curricular knowledge about Brazil, especially in relation to the black population, favoring the construction of positive identity references for the Brazilian population (FELIPE & TERUYA, 2010, p.14).

The contributions of historical knowledge are linked to the importance of societies understanding the present. This allows citizens to perceive themselves as active subjects and producers of history, understanding that today's problems have been historically constructed. Lima (2004) also points out that:

> Since the dawn of the construction of knowledge about human societies, it

> has been known that elaborating and making sense of a people's history means giving them the tools to form their own identity, using the raw material of that identity, which is their social memory (p.160).

With regard to the problems related to racism and racial inequalities in Brazil, historical knowledge on the subject can contribute to understanding the historical process, from the genesis to the maintenance of these problems, and thus provide subsidies for mitigating or resolving them through the articulation between the problematization of the present and the historical process. The various forms of violence to which black people are currently subjected in Brazil are the result of this black history, which began in Africa and continued to be produced from the diaspora onwards, segregating, subordinating and socially excluding black people. It is through a historiographical approach and a critical reading of this history, black history, that teachers will be able to help build a new consciousness that strives for respect, equality and social justice.

2.2 - On art teaching and the racial issue

When we talk about the arts, we are referring to the many forms of artistic expression, such as the visual arts, theater, music and dance. Art consists of practices that have been part of the experiences of human beings since the first forms of organization of social groups on the planet, often related to religiosity, the production of utensils, tools, sculptures, buildings and records that signified forms of communication. Corroborating this interpretation, Figueiredo (1991) reports that art is:

> The expression of an idea, an emotion, a feeling, through images and symbols. Art teaches us about life in all its dimensions and is everything that delights our eyes and touches our hearts. Art can be a painting, a sculpture, a pen drawing, a symphony, a text (p. 03).

Through the arts, people can express their culture, their identity and their social relations. In this way, art as a personal and cultural expression contributes to the perception of different ways of life and social progress. Article 26 - 2 of LDB 9394/96 states that "art teaching will be a compulsory curricular component at all levels of basic education, in order to promote students' cultural development". In this sense, art/education (art in educational spaces) is an important educational tool, as it stimulates intelligence, creativity and allows forms of communication and social interaction to be established through other languages. Barbosa (1998) states that a:

> Reading works of art is questioning, searching, discovering, and awakening critical capacity [...] a critical education of knowledge built by the student themselves, with the teacher's mediation, about the visual world, and not a banking education (p. 40).

Art/education can also help to bring students into contact with other spaces and environments, interacting with other cultures, thus opening up possibilities for valuing diversity. Barbosa (2008) tells us that:

> Art enables man not to be a stranger in his foreign environment or a foreigner in his own country. It overcomes the state of depersonalization, inserting the individual in the place where they belong, reinforcing and expanding their place in the world. Art in education, as both personal and cultural expression, is an important tool for cultural identification and individual development (p. 99).

In this way, art/education must contribute to the ethical formation and emancipation of the subject, by means of a critical stance on the part of educators, the curricula and the political-pedagogical projects of the institutions, distancing art teaching from a pedagogical practice devoid of meaning.

When it comes to studying race relations through black history and culture, the school subject of art education is one of the priorities for working with this theme. In this process, art can play an important role in the process of valuing African culture and recognizing its influences on Brazilian culture, as Hernandëz (2000, p.261) states: "in order to understand the art of a people, it is necessary to see their works not as something isolated, but to know the culture from which they come". Because, not unlike other curricular components of basic education, there has historically been a prevalent Eurocentric tendency in arts content, guided by a significant presence of artistic productions from Europe and a neglect of artistic manifestations of black origin.

Art is based on culture and assimilates it as one of the main factors conditioning the social actions of individuals and groups. In view of this, meaningful pedagogical practice in art/education can help students understand the relationship between culture and power and its implications for the society in which they live. Right:

> All classes have the right to access the codes of erudite culture, because these are the codes of the dominant culture - the codes of power. It is necessary to know them, to be well versed in them, but these codes will remain external knowledge unless the individual has mastered the cultural references of their own social class, the gateway to assimilation of the "other". Social mobility depends on the interrelationship between the cultural codes of the different social classes and understanding the world depends on a broad vision that integrates the erudite and the popular. (BARBOSA, 2003, p. 20)

To this end, it is the art teacher's responsibility to take care not to reproduce stereotypical views when working with the themes established by Law 10.639/03 at school, in order to create a new view of cultural diversity by recognizing and understanding the visual codes present. In this sense, in the search for an Artistic Education that contributes to the education of racial relations and anti-racism, Silva (2008) presents some objectives for the teaching of different artistic languages. With regard to the teaching of theater, the author highlights:

> Rescuing Afro-Brazilian culture in order to reintegrate students into the ethnic and social values of their national ancestry; getting the student to learn about African aesthetic concepts; facilitating the construction of the student's identity through positive self-identification with themselves and with Brazil's historical and cultural heritage; and getting the student to critically recognize the stereotypes of ethnic representation found in the Performing Arts in general and in Brazilian theater in particular (p.125).

For the teaching of Visual Arts, the concerns pointed out by the author are:

> By means of the Visual Arts, we can rescue African cultural ancestry/actuality; we can make students aware of African aesthetic concepts; we can enable students to identify themselves as a person in the group; and we can make students critically recognize the stereotypes of ethnic representation found in the Visual Arts, in advertising and in the media in general (SILVA, 2008, p.129).

As for the teaching of music in schools, the author states that it is important:

> Valuing the students' identity; disrespecting the student's creative sensibility; getting the students to collectively build their own material; getting the students to get to know other ethnic and cultural groups; and getting the students to recover their knowledge of African influences on Brazilian art (SILVA, 2008, p.133).

Silva (2008) highlights the importance of teaching danga:

> By means of Danga, we can rescue African cultural ancestry/actuality; lead students to recognize the capacities and limits of their bodies; develop cognitive and motor aspects and body harmony; develop students' collective spirit; and develop students' creativity (p.136).

With these objectives in mind, we stress that art teaching must therefore observe the culture of origin of the students' previous knowledge, while at the same time stimulating their desire to get to know other cultures and artistic productions, contributing to the democratization of access to cultural production, given that only an education that values cultural diversity can be understood as democratic. Because, according to the objectives set out in the PCN for Art, the role of this subject is to provide students with:

> To know and value the plurality of Brazil's socio-cultural heritage, as well as the socio-cultural aspects of other peoples and nations, opposing any discrimination based on different cultures, social class, beliefs, gender, ethnicity or other individual and social characteristics. (BRASIL, 1997, p.7)

We can consider art and culture as intrinsic elements, where any curricular content that deals with the correspondence between art and black culture, in this case in art teaching, can guarantee an understanding of this diversity as a constituent element of our society and culture. By describing the context of the various artistic productions through art/education, it creates the possibility of understanding the historical facts linked to the different artistic patterns that have emerged throughout the history of black peoples, contributing to building respect for this diversity. In this way, the Arts subject is a fundamental part of the fight against prejudice and racial discrimination in education and society.

2.3 - On the teaching of literature and the issue of race

Literature is of fundamental importance in the formative processes of individuals. Working with literature in schools should stimulate curiosity and pleasure in reading, contributing to the development of a critical sense, the ability to interpret, as well as improving writing skills. As Candido (1972, apud PARANA, 2008) states, literature is the art that transforms, that is, humanizes human beings and society. Literature as a human production is intrinsically linked to social life.

Through literature, values inherent to society are disseminated, so it is necessary for basic education to break away from traditional Eurocentric curricular organizations in order to take into account Brazil's human and cultural diversity. This will help to establish humanizing social values, thus exercising the social function of literature, which is a way for us to get to know the world, history, peoples and cultures. Alencar et al (2008, p. 132) point out that:

> Literary works, while representing social relations, are also capable of reshaping and restructuring social practices, contributing to discursive change by presenting new forms, new meanings and, consequently, contributing to social change.

It's in this context that we think about the importance of including black literature[3] in primary school classrooms. Because this is a significant space for confronting ideas, thoughts and social values that intersect, where it is possible to establish possibilities for repositioning elitist, ethnocentric, discriminatory and segregationist social paradigms through critical reading. But what constitutes or defines black literature? Espinheira-Filho (2013, p.73) contributes to elucidating this issue by stating that:

> The dynamics and scope of literature allow us to name it or specify it according to the aesthetic or discursive positioning of those who create it, or the group it is aimed at or produces for. It is common to find some specific denominations, such as women's literature, Bahian literature, Brazilian literature, English literature, marginal literature, among many others. It is important to emphasize that these names do not affect the nature of literary art. They merely demarcate the territory of a particular group who, in space and time, needed or need to situate themselves as voices linked to a specific identity, or who want to be visible on the cultural and social scene.

In this sense, black literature consists of literature that, according to Fonseca (2006), addresses "issues relating to the identity and cultures of African and Afro-descendant peoples" (p.11), which, in turn, "by seeking to integrate itself into the struggles for awareness of the black population, seeks to give meaning to processes of identity formation of groups excluded from the social model thought up by our

---

[3] We have chosen here to use the term "black literature" and not "Afro-Brazilian literature" or "Afro-descendant literature", understanding that the term "Afro-Brazilian" refers to the segments of Afro-origin existing only in Brazil, thus not contemplating African literature and the literature of black segments from other parts of the world. The term "Afro-descendant", on the other hand, refers to a question of descent and is not necessarily related to what defines what it means to be black, especially in the Brazilian perception, such as phenotype and identity and their implications for the occurrence of racial discrimination. In this way, we agree that "The use of expressions such as 'Afro-Brazilian' and 'Afro-descendant' seeks to dilute the essentialism contained in the expression 'black literature' and overcome the difficulty of characterizing this literature without taking on the complex discussions raised by the Negritude movement at another historical moment" (FONSECA, 2006, p.38).

society" (p.2324).

In this way, the deconstruction of traditional values through a new look at literature is necessary in this process of searching for cultural transformation, because, as Silva (2010) reports, "in Brazilian literature, the black person is an excluded word, often forgotten, or a representation invented by the other, in general the marginal element" (p.01). In this sense, it is necessary to build new perspectives on the person and the word "black".

Possibly a major challenge for the development of work with black literature is the difficulty in defining which works are part of it.
literary framework. Also according to Silva (2010, p.02):

> The criteria used to define Black or Afro-Brazilian Literature are a controversial topic that precedes and sometimes surpasses the analysis of the literary works themselves. Among the various criteria used to define this literature, the following have been considered: ethnic criteria (which link the work to the author's black or mixed-race origin) and thematic criteria (which identify content of Afro-Brazilian origin as characterizing Black or Afro-Brazilian Literature). [...] these criteria are not very comprehensive, since we can observe the fact that, throughout Brazil's literary formation, we have had black and mixed-race writers writing according to classical European standards, as well as non-black writers writing about themes of Afro-Brazilian interest such as slavery, the revolt of the quilombolas and racial prejudice.

In an attempt to understand the contributions of this literature to the critical formation of subjects from a perspective of diversity, the author analyzed a set of books on Afro-Brazilian literature, and found that they addressed the following issues

> [...] the symbolism, the mythology and the return to nature, so many teachings and a whole sacredness contained in the stories that can contribute to the formation of the individual, enabling them to become more loving towards themselves, others and nature (SILVA, 2010, p.02).

The cultural contributions and traditions of black peoples can no longer be denied in Brazil, diluting them in the idea of miscegenation of peoples, or by their supposed agglutination, which has been disseminated by the discourse linked to the myth of racial democracy.

Thus, working with black literature is an essential way of combating anti-racism in education, of building an affirmative view of black history and culture in

Brazil, of recognizing the multiple identities that are part of the school environment and of improving the self-esteem of black students, because "the sense of who we are is constructed narratively" (LARROSA, 1996, p.147). To do this, it is necessary to use didactic and paradidactic materials that are in line with the specificity of the theme dealt with here. Souza & Lima (2006) report that:

> [...] books that take up traces and symbols of Afro-Brazilian culture, such as religions of African origin, capoeira, dance and the mechanisms of resistance against discrimination, with the aim of providing positive stimulation and favorable self-esteem for black readers and a possibility of representation that allows non-black readers to get in touch with another side of Afro-Brazilian culture that is still little explored at school, in the media, as well as in society in general (p. 216).

Thus, in order for the teaching of black literature to help build human values and transform them into social practices, it is necessary to properly include these materials and contents in basic education curricula. As Silva (2010) points out:

> In the light of Afro-Brazilian tales, it is possible to recover the myths and provoke teachers and learners to take a new look at their identification in the field of different masks: at work, in the family and at school, in view of the lack of desire to glimpse the magical and symbolic world in nature itself (p.05).

Efforts must also be made in this direction on the part of education management bodies, institutions that promote teacher training, schools and, above all, teachers, so that, through literature, the ethnocentric values that are rooted in people's mentalities in our society can be stirred up, in order to make them more sensitive to issues related to interracial relations and diversity.

3 - THE CONCEPT OF "RACE" AND THE TEACHING OF NATURAL SCIENCES AND SOCIOLOGY FOR UNDERSTANDING RACIAL ISSUES

According to Guimaraes (2003), "raga" is a concept that "has at least two analytical meanings: one claimed by genetic biology and the other by sociology" (p.95). According to this author:

> Biology and physical anthropology created the idea of human races, i.e. the idea that the human species could be divided into subspecies, just like the animal world, and that this division would be associated with the differential development of moral values, psychic and intellectual gifts among human beings. To be honest, this was science for a while and only then did it become pseudoscience. We all know that what we call racism wouldn't exist without this idea that divides human beings into races, into subspecies, each with their own qualities. It was this idea that hierarchized human societies and populations and founded a certain doctrinaire racism (Guimaraes, 2003, p.95-96).

It was this biological conception of race that supported the development of eugenicist theories, a study that according to Diwan (2007) "acquired a scientific status and aimed to implement a method of human selection based on biological premises" (p.10), which served as the basis for the legitimization of racism and consequently for the production and reproduction of inequalities and other forms of racialized violence that exist in many societies. In this sense, Guimaraes (2003) argues that:

> [...] ragas are, scientifically, a social construction and should be studied by a branch of sociology or social sciences that deals with social identities. We are thus in the field of culture, and symbolic culture. We can say that "ragas" are the effects of discourses (p.96).

With this in mind, we have raised the importance of critically historicizing the development of the Natural Sciences and the racial theories they disseminate, adopting a critical perspective that seeks reflection and understanding in relation to economic and group interests, i.e. who these theories and the knowledge they produce served and what their logics were throughout their historical development. This seems to us to be a good way to insert the racial debate into the agenda of the Natural Sciences, both as a body of science and as school subjects.

As a curricular component of basic education, the Natural Sciences, more than just providing the teaching of systematized knowledge, must contribute to the integral formation of the student, to the exercise of citizenship, results that depend primarily on the performance and clear commitment of teachers in these areas to their pedagogical work. In this sense, Santos (2006, p. 01, apud. SILVA, 2009, p.15) points out that:

> Today's attention in education is basically focused on the idea of citizenship and the training of teachers with new professional profiles, masters who are able to work with an interdisciplinary view of science, appropriate to the multiple ways of knowing and intervening in society today.

Also, the PCN - National Curriculum Parameters for the teaching of Natural Sciences states that the objectives of the teaching of Natural Sciences "are designed to enable students to develop skills that allow them to understand the world and act as individuals and citizens, using knowledge of a scientific and technological nature" (BRASIL, 1997).

Sociology, with Emile Durkheim (1858-1917) as one of its main exponents, sought to systematize and give substance to this science, assigning it the "social facts" as its object of investigation. Social facts consist of everything that is socially imposed on human beings, such as culture, values, rules and laws. Thus, in Durkheim's conception, sociology is responsible for investigating social facts, seeking to understand the "complex interweaving of all the intricate patterns of human social relations" (Morrish, 1975, p.17).

Understanding how society is organized and the social relationships within it is of fundamental importance if people are to perceive themselves as members of society, identifying the positions they occupy within it. The study of sociology opens up ways of understanding social differences, exclusion, segregation, invisibility and the various forms of violence that certain social groups are subjected to.

Understanding education from a perspective of integral formation, as a process of humanization, knowing that, while it promotes conservation, it can also promote revolution, taking into account the determinations that occur in the relationships between human beings and society, through their mutual influences, and that the study of Sociology becomes essential for the construction of a critical and citizen consciousness.

This awareness can provide the basis for the emancipation of subjects and the development of citizen participation in the quest to build a truly democratic society. Morrish (1975, p.31) points out that:

> As a discipline, sociology has taught us how to find out; it has taught us not to accept any of the social influences as axiomatic facts, but to consider the social environment as a set of patterns to be explored according to their educational significance.

On the basis of these explanations, we can return to the discussion about the role that the Natural Sciences and Biology can play in promoting education for racial relations. In order to be able to think about education for race relations in science teaching, we will initially establish a summary of what science teaching is about and the reasons for its inclusion and permanence in the official curricula of basic education schools in Brazil. On this subject, Silva (2009, p.11) points out that:

> [...] the term "science teaching" is used in relation to school practice dedicated to the teaching and learning of scientific knowledge and its social impact. More specifically, knowledge produced in the field of Natural Sciences, organized in the school system in the form of subjects: Natural Sciences, in Primary School and Biology; Physics and Chemistry in Secondary School.

With the responsibility attributed to science teaching in mind, we bring up the issue of education for racial relations, especially with regard to the history and culture of black peoples. Silva (2009) raises some questions that contribute to this discussion:

> Bearing in mind that science teaching should educate citizens, and considering the important role of ethnic-racial relations in promoting this citizenship, one might ask: how can science teaching contribute to this? How can teachers teach with this orientation? Are science teachers prepared for this task? (.p.18)

These are questions that open up a series of investigations, given that scientific production in the field of race relations in science teaching is still not very significant, which demonstrates the little attention given to the theme in the body of this curricular component, as well as the importance of seeking spaces for the theme to become a significant agenda in the teaching of Natural Sciences. In this sense, Verrangia (2009 apud VERRANGIA 2013) points out that:

> Science teaching, like all curricular components, plays an important role in

> promoting ethical social relationships among students. Unfortunately, ethno-racial diversity is still not considered a central issue in the training of teachers in this area, either initial or continuing (p.107).

Based on these findings, we think about the challenges for science teaching to take into account and contribute to the establishment of an education for racial relations, because as Silva (2009) points out:

> The frequent uncritical teaching and learning of science engages teachers and students in the maintenance of racism. This is because science teaching incorporates a form of subtle racist propaganda that is difficult to detect, especially given that this form of knowledge is commonly perceived as politically neutral (p.12).

It is therefore necessary to look for strategies to re-read the ways in which science teaching is approached. However, much still needs to be done to make this specificity a reality. A first step is to recognize these needs and, above all, to be open to dialogue with other types of knowledge and to research, because as Silva (2009) also points out:

> Faced with this need to produce science teaching that is effectively committed to combating racism, there is an almost total absence of specific guidelines, both from the government and from the literature on science education and teaching in Brazil. This absence does not prevent us from seeking to understand how current legislation and literature in the area contribute, or not, to the development of such teaching. This understanding necessarily involves discussing the relationship between science teaching and citizenship (p.13).

Another way forward is to rescue the natural sciences and their knowledge, which has historically been neglected by the history of science as scientific knowledge. I'm talking about the science that was practiced in Africa long before the European colonial onslaughts on the continent. In addition, it is also important to carry out surveys of what is being produced in these areas today and to make this knowledge curriculum content in the classrooms of Brazilian schools. Teachers can play a fundamental role in this process. Verrangia (2013) points out that:

> [...] with a view to educating for the full exercise of citizenship, it is necessary for science teachers, teacher trainers and researchers to ask themselves about concrete ways in which this teaching can contribute to the appreciation of African and Afro-Brazilian history and culture (p.107).

Just as human beings emerged on the African continent, so too did scientific production in the most varied fields of knowledge, and this is no different for the natural sciences. This is how human beings and their knowledge spread from Africa to the world. Recognizing this and taking this perspective into educational spheres signals a new path for race relations in education and for the commitment of Natural Science teaching to the democratization of knowledge, culture and society.

Thus, with regard to racial issues, overcoming the conflicts, inequalities and violence caused by racism is of fundamental importance if racial equality is to be achieved in Brazil. But for this to happen, there needs to be increasingly expressive mobilization around these issues. Sociologist Karl Mannheim (1893-1947) believed that:

> [...] if a democratic society invested as much energy and time in mitigating racial and group hatred as totalitarian societies had invested in fomenting it, important achievements could thus be made in eliminating conflict. (Morrish, 1975, p.30)

In recent decades, the field of sociology has seen significant and growing scientific production focused on racial issues in Brazil. Here we need to reflect on school knowledge and on the contributions of this knowledge to a pedagogical practice in the teaching of sociology focused on race relations and anti-racism. This is where the challenge arises, from this perspective, of thinking about the pedagogical dimension of Sociology in the movement to recompose values. In this sense, Oliveira (2014) reports that:

> If, on the one hand, there is a tradition of studies on the racial question in Brazil within the social sciences, on the other, there is still extreme difficulty in transposing these discussions into the educational field and, in the specific case of sociology teaching, the impasses and tensions are greater given the trajectory of this subject in basic education (p.82).

Sociology as a compulsory subject in basic education is still a recent development, and came about through Law 11.684 of 2008, which made it compulsory only in secondary education. For this reason, "the social sciences still lack school tradition and knowledge about their object of study by a large part of the subjects present at school" (OLIVEIRA, 2014, p.82).

It is up to sociologists, sociology teachers and other educational thinkers to find ways in which sociology teaching can contribute to achieving the objectives of an education focused on racial relations. To do this, according to Oliveira (2014, p.82), it is necessary to:

> [...] the affirmation of a new epistemological stance on race relations in Brazil and the attempt to build school knowledge in sociology based on the new epistemological foundations of historical knowledge on race relations.

Based on these developments in the teaching of Natural Sciences and Sociology and education on race relations, we tried to show that this is a pertinent topic for these two school subjects, highlighting the role they play in promoting the objectives of an education based on an integral formation for the exercise of citizenship.

4 - GEOGRAPHY TEACHING AND RACIAL RELATIONS IN THE GEOGRAPHICAL SPACE

In order to think about the possible contributions of geography teaching and racial issues, we consider it valid to take as a starting point some questions put forward by Vazzoler (2006):

> What geographical knowledge can be considered essential for interdisciplinary geography? How can these studies contribute to improving people's lives? How can we live with spatial discrimination without questioning the imposition of an exclusionary society? How has the school positioned itself in the face of the legal requirements that determine teaching/learning that is close to the students? (p.26).

We understand Geography as the science of space, which studies the relationships that are dialectically established between human beings and nature, thus being concerned with analyzing the social relationships that are established in the most varied locations on the planet and which take place on and/or from a physical material base. As Calai (2013) states, the problems of space are the problems of human beings and society, which materialize in space. Based on these spatial perceptions, it is possible to say that geography is a social science (DAMIANI, 1999). Santos (2010) reports that:

> The idea that Geography is used to get to know the world, and to know about the world, is always present in speeches and common sense. More than that, Geography contributes to human formation, providing references for the individual's insertion in the world, in their socialization spaces. [...] Knowing Geography means knowing where you are, knowing the world, but this is fundamentally for you to act on that world in the process of rebuilding society: to present yourself in order to participate (p.142-143).

In order to better understand the role of Geography in educational processes, we have adopted a different approach:

> [...] a theoretical perspective that considers the distinction between scientific geography and school geography. Discarding the idea of a simple didactic (or curricular) transposition, it is necessary to discuss what is taught geography and geographic science (CALAI, 2013, p.76).

According to Calai (2013) School Geography corresponds to the social function of Geography. According to the author:

> Several scholars working on research into the teaching of geography consider that school geography does not identify with academic geography,

> although this is the basic source of its legitimacy. It is understood that from the benchmarks of academic geography, the benchmarks for school geography are established, and this is the geographic knowledge that is actually worked on in the classroom. Based on this statement and moving forward, it can be emphasized that school geography is the result of selecting which content to work on based on what is specific to the science of geography, but which is defined by the parameters of the school, considering its context. In this way, new school-specific knowledge is produced (CALAI, 2013, p.76).

Thus, working with school geography, especially given its pedagogical dimension, should provide students with "an understanding of the reality in which we live, from the perspective of a spatial viewpoint" (Calai, 2013, p.105). In this sense, through a reading of the world based on an analysis of the geographical space, it contributes to the critical formation of students and prepares them to exercise their citizenship. Damiani (1999) contributes to this reflection by stating that:

> The notion of citizenship involves a sense of place and space, since it is the materialization of relationships of all kinds, whether close or distant. Knowing one's space means knowing the network of relationships to which one is subject, of which one is subject. The alienation of space and citizenship constitute an antagonism to be considered (p.50).

The processes of production and reproduction of geographical spaces take place in the midst of various tensions resulting from the unequal relationships that exist in society, often linked to the exploitation and segregation of social, economic, ethnic and racial groups. In Brazil, the shaping of the territory and the people also bears these characteristics.

In this way, we can say that the history of race relations in Brazil is essentially geographical, as it is directly related to the configuration of the Brazilian geographical space, as it is marked by processes of territorialization, deterritorialization and reterritorialization, socio-spatial segregation, the construction of identities and feelings of belonging to places, which directly influences many of the regional socio-cultural characteristics and the configuration of a multitude of landscapes, whether urban or not. According to Porto-Gongalves (2006):

> [...] a society that constitutes its relations through racism, has in its geography places and spaces with the marks of this social distinction: in the Brazilian case, the black population is a clear majority in prisons and an absolute minority in universities (p. 11).

From this analysis it is possible to see, as Santos (2011) states, that "raga becomes, from this point of view, a geographical concept, a notion that is based on spatial readings" (p. 11). In this sense, Vazzoler (2006) adds that:

> Geography is currently concerned with explaining the network of relationships that take place in the geographical space that makes up the landscape, starting from an understanding of the social and racial relationships situated in the geographical space. In order to achieve justice and democracy, thus envisioning a new way of constructing space, it is necessary to discuss spatial organization (p.29).

However, the analysis of spatial relations, whose main markers are racial issues, has not yet received adequate attention in academic geography. Ratts (2004) reports that:

> Geography has historically focused more on pointing out the spatial distribution of ethnic-racial segments than on carrying out an analysis that conceives of race and ethnicity as structuring categories of social relations that have spatiality as one of the basic aspects of their constitution (p. 82).

Currently, it is possible to find a growing amount of work in the field of Geography focused on racial issues. In this sense, a researcher who carried out a study on racial production in Geography found the following after his survey:

> [...] we find four trends that make up the geographical discussions on the ethnic-racial question, [...]. They are: space and ethno-racial relations; black identities and territorialities; geopolitics of African countries; and cultural and religious territories and manifestations (CIRQUEIRA & CORREA, 2012, p. 09).

Even though black cultural traditions are gradually gaining notoriety on the academic scene. A problem also raised with regard to studies on race relations in Geography is the fact that a significant proportion of research does not contribute to unveiling the racism and racial hierarchies that exist in our society. Contributing to this reflection, I bring up Ratts' (2004) notes that:

> Although the amount of research on ethnic-racial issues in geography is high, few works have sought to denounce the way in which geographical science has reproduced a discourse that reinforces the superiority of some races and ethnicities over others (p. 82).

In this sense, it is important to raise the role of Geography as a science, but especially as a school subject for the construction of an anti-racist education, and the importance of a new positioning of Geography in the face of Law 10.639/03, because as Vazzoler (2006) states:

> [...] the study of geography can offer, within a school institution, a debate on a multitude of issues, including racial issues, based on the object of study of this discipline, which is the production of space, built by different peoples, with all its conflicts and tensions (p. 15).

Santos (2011) also defends the idea that "Geography teaching can be an instrument of education for racial equality" (p. 05). Thus, according to Santos (2010) "if we believe that raga is an element that regulates social relations, somehow its manifestations are imbricated in Geography [...] [because] The regulation of social relations operated from the idea of raga has a direct relationship with space" (p.144).

However, more than ten years have passed since the enactment of Law 10.639 and its results in school environments still seem to be underwhelming, even when it comes to working with the subjects that are said to be priorities for working with the Law (History, Literature and Arts), further highlighting the need for Geography to make room for attention to education on race relations. This is undoubtedly still a long job to be done, but if it is carried out with the proper attention and involvement of geographic science and school geography, major contributions can be made to anti-racism and the construction of racial equality.

For this to happen, it is above all necessary for primary school teachers to practice a curriculum in Geography teaching that includes a critical reading of spatialized racial relations, so that school Geography contributes to compliance with Law 10.639/03, but also contributes to the achievement of the objectives of education, in terms of preparing the subjects in formation for the full exercise of citizenship.

It is also necessary to analyze what needs to be done to make this anti-racist education a reality, to think about "what the conditions are, what the challenges are for an educational practice and for geography teaching that is committed to promoting racial equality" (SANTOS, 2011, p.08). These issues involve various components, such as initial and continuing teacher training, official curricula and the teaching materials available. Among these materials are textbooks, which have an effective presence in school environments and for students represent a scientific character as the bearer of truth, and also in many cases the only books that students have access to.

According to Tonini (2000):

> The textbook, as a field of knowledge production, is shaped by relations of power that constitute the geographical discourses it contains. It is the product of a place that shapes it through countless processes and agents. The geographical knowledge recorded there, formalized as knowledge, is what is being worked on at school. I try to show through this cultural artifact - the textbook - how geographical discourses come into play in teaching to legitimize the construction of ethnic identities, maintaining and perpetuating forms of meaning (p. 02).

By focusing his attention on the racial issue in Geography textbooks, through a synthesis of various studies analyzing textbooks, one researcher found that "research indicates little participation by blacks; however, simply including them in Geography textbooks may not be enough to overcome certain forms of racial hierarchization" (SANTOS, 2014, p. 07). In this sense, according to Vazzoler (2006):

> If one of the functions of geography is to indicate new directions, nothing could be fairer than to include in its studies themes that deal with problems for which society has not yet found a solution, such as racism, the marginalization of certain social sectors, and many others. Since the issue of racism and the marginalization of the black population is a problem that interferes with the social relations that take place in the geographical space, wouldn't this be a topic that should be covered in textbooks and included in the geography syllabus? (p.79).

These surveys show that we are still some way from being able to comprehensively perceive school geography acting in the direction of anti-racist education. But for this to happen, it is necessary to work with the different social actors in search of a geography education focused on racial relations. We believe, as Werthein (2002) states, that "education can change values, contributing to the appreciation of diversity and the building of a sense of mutual respect between the groups that make up this rich geography of cultural identities called Brazil" (p. 10). Thus, as Vazzoler (2006) points out:

> What can we teachers do to ensure that, through the study of geography, our students learn about the human condition of black people, discover their own value as active agents in society and acquire the ability to critically analyze the unequal treatment of black people? Firstly, addressing these aspects does not mean inventing new content; rather, it is proposed that, when discussing the concepts and content offered by geography, the teacher breaks with the traditional approach to the themes to be studied (p.18-19).

From a re-reading of what concerns the specificities of school geography and its attention to racial issues, we believe that in order to achieve an education for racial relations, in the search for the consolidation of a critical notion of citizenship, the teaching of geography can also articulate its knowledge with that of other disciplines, thus enabling an interdisciplinary reading of the racial relations that permeate Brazil.

5 - PHYSICAL EDUCATION TEACHING HAS A LOT TO CONTRIBUTE TO RACE RELATIONS EDUCATION

The reflections contained here start from what defines School Physical Education, its importance in the formative process in basic education and its possible contributions to the application of Law 10.639/03 in school environments. We then looked for a conceptualization of this curricular discipline and according to CONFER - the Federal Council for Physical Education:

> School Physical Education is understood as a discipline that introduces and integrates the student into the body culture of movement, forming the citizen who will produce, reproduce and transform it, enabling them to use games, sports, dances, fights and gymnastics to the benefit of the critical exercise of citizenship and the improvement of quality of life (2002, p.04).

Thus contributing to the individual's understanding of themselves, the culture they are part of and other cultures through work on three blocks which, according to the PCN for Physical Education, are: games, gymnastics, sports and wrestling; rhythmic and expressive activities; and knowledge about the body. In addition to working on its specific characteristics, Physical Education at school must establish interdisciplinary relationships with other subjects in the school curriculum, in order to integrate school knowledge with the experiences of the social groups that are part of the school environment.

But in order for this to happen, it is necessary to break with traditional educational practices that are rooted in the perception of Physical Education teaching, which according to CONFER (2002, p.05) is "geared towards the formation of sports teams representing the schools, seen by students as a recreational practice, as a way of breaking the time of intellectual teaching". Strategies need to be sought so that School Physical Education produces another "reading and understanding different from the one we are shown as being a segregationist, elitist, exclusionary discipline promoted through stereotyped exercises" (idem. p.07). Thus allowing it to become:

> [...] a subject within the pedagogical and formative context of citizenship, with the aim of explaining corporeality, the meaning of quality of life through an active lifestyle, which offers some thematic experiences so that students can try out exercises and practices. The discipline cannot be based

> on or justified by practice, but rather by its purpose (CONFER, 2002, p.09).

Thus, when we refer to the study of black history and culture in Physical Education, we are talking about the study of race relations in the field of Body Culture, understood as:

> [...] a totality formed by the interaction of different social practices, such as dance, games, gymnastics and sport, which, in turn, materialize, take shape, through bodily practices. As social practices, they reflect the productive human activity of seeking answers to its needs (CASTELLANI-FILHO, 1998, p.54).

According to Oliveira (2004), Physical Education identifies itself with the human and social sciences, taking on a pedagogical-social stance that gives it unsurpassed dignity. Through this prism and the construction of values and movements related to the body, it is possible to understand the racial relations that are established in our country and beyond. In this sense, Castellani-Filho (1998, p.54) reports that "it is therefore up to Physical Education to give pedagogical treatment to the themes of body culture, recognizing them as endowed with meaning and sense because they are historically constructed".

In order to rethink the relationship, we think it's necessary to revisit some issues that have permeated the history of Physical Education in Brazil, linked to the eugenicist thinking that spread in the country, especially from the end of the 19th century and the beginning of the 20th century. The eugenicist theories sought to spread the idea in society that the biological characteristics of individuals (especially color/race) were conditioning factors for the physical and moral aspects of human beings, in other words, human qualities were more related to biological succession than to the education received. It would thus consist of a science that sought to improve the qualities of a race or a people.

These thoughts fostered the development of hygienist policies in Brazilian society, such as the attraction of European migrants after the abolition of slavery with the aim of whitening the Brazilian population. It also led to the establishment of views and values about certain segments of the population and two cultures, above all blacks and indigenous people. In this way, "the science of eugenics provided a bridge between racial ideology and popular culture, defining a culture of poverty" (D'AVILA, 2006, p.93). Based on these assumptions, Moreira (et. al., 2009) reports that:

> The foundations of the historical construction of Physical Education favored eugenicist interests. Aside from the pedagogical process, the French and Swedish methods of gymnastics, which were widely disseminated in Brazil, were effective for the ideals of a mechanical and disciplined body. Sport, in turn, embraced the idea of white superiority, supported by the mythologically aspired Hellenic body image (p.06).

This highlights the racist perspective that permeated the work with Physical Education, through the relationships established between the discipline and the black body. For, as Mattos (2007, p.11) states, "the history of the discipline of Physical Education points to a distancing from the black body, insofar as the body idealized by Physical Education was based on the body image of the Greeks, therefore a white body".

According to Moreira (et. al., 2009, p.10) "the study of ethno-racial relations in physical education should lead to a reflection on the body and power and reveal the extent to which these relations have influenced the production of racist stereotypes". According to Mattos (2007, p.11), deconstructing this thinking and attitude in physical education is "a complex challenge, considering that the ideals of beauty are based on an imaginary constructed from white aesthetics".

Moreira (et. al., 2009, p.09) further reinforces the role of Physical Education in understanding racial relations from a pedagogical perspective by making the following statement:

> [...] in contemporary times, the great struggle of education is aimed at enriching praxis from the perspective of breaking down prejudices and respecting origins, identities and cultures, the great task, therefore, of physical education is to fight to be empowered in the process.

In this sense, it is hoped that in the construction of curricula and pedagogical proposals for School Physical Education, the social implications that have been created and reproduced as a result of racism will be observed, such as racial inequalities, the segregation of cultures and limitations in relation to access to education, as well as reflection and action based on a Body Culture that takes racial diversity into account.

Moreira (et. al., 2009, p.11-12) also reports that "with the advent of Law No. 10.639/03, a re-reading of the body and society has become urgent, as well as other readings on black and indigenous corporeality and movement in the field of body culture". The author adds that it is necessary:

> "observing the state of 'critical interculturality' in the practice of Physical Education as a way of facing up to the challenges of implementing Law 10.639/03 insofar as these strategies can become equitable to the values of the manifestations of body culture at school" (p.11-12).

A lot still needs to be done in the field of Physical Education and Body Culture to develop work that values black history and culture. To do this, teachers need to recognize the importance of inserting body practices with African roots in a contextualized way, thus giving them meaning and enabling a dialogue and learning that respects diversity.

6 - IS THERE ROOM FOR RACE RELATIONS IN MATHEMATICS TEACHING?

Thinking about the function of mathematics education involves a certain complexity, given that there is no consensus among professionals and thinkers who deal with mathematics teaching, as Miguel (2005, p.376) reports, "the thesis of education as a universal value historically places the discussion about the production and dissemination of mathematical knowledge, in particular, as a pendulum that, in general, oscillates between objectivism and subjectivism". In other words, does the teaching of mathematics aim at mathematical development or mathematical learning on the part of the student? To this, the author adds that "this dichotomy between development and learning has consequences for the organization of teaching programs and for the methodological way in which mathematical knowledge is disseminated" (2005, p.376). According to Vigostky (1998, p. 118):

> [...] learning is not development; however, properly organized learning results in mental development and sets in motion various developmental processes that would otherwise be impossible. Thus, learning is a necessary and universal aspect of the development process of culturally organized and specifically human psychological functions.

Learning mathematics is about more than equipping students to perform logical operations, to work with numbers and mathematical operations in a decontextualized way. Not that these technical operational skills aren't important, but in view of the purpose of school education, the teaching of mathematics should contribute to the development of a reading of the world, enabling the interpretation of multiple contexts and at different scales of observation. Miguel (2005, p.376-377) points out that:

> In fact, mathematical knowledge is not consolidated as a list of ideas ready to be memorized; much moreover, a meaningful mathematics teaching process must lead students to explore a wide variety of ideas and establish relationships between facts and concepts in order to incorporate real-world contexts, experiences and the natural way of engaging in the development of mathematical notions with a view to acquiring different ways of perceiving reality. But we still need to make progress in terms of guiding children to understand the evolution of mathematical ideas, gradually broadening their understanding of them.

It is therefore necessary to understand the dialectical relationship between learning and development, where the former enables the latter to occur and thus creates the conditions for the former to occur again at a more advanced level. "Failure to pay adequate attention to the relationship between development and learning has consequences for teaching concepts and their implications for pedagogical practice" (MIGUEL, 2005, p.377).

In this way, we believe that mathematics should be taught in a contextualized way, because mathematics is part of students' various everyday experiences. Understanding mathematics, or understanding the world from a mathematical perspective, can enable new ways of reading and interpreting reality, problems and everyday situations. Miguel (2005, p.377) also contributes to this interpretation by pointing out that:

> Beyond the scientific and technological dimensions, mathematics has become a fundamental component of the general culture of the citizen, which can be observed in everyday language, in the press, in laws, in advertising, in games, in jokes and in many other everyday situations.

Mathematics is inserted into the contexts of the most varied social groupings, having its own arrangements and historical development in order to meet the needs of these societies and, to this end, this mathematical knowledge is articulated with knowledge from other areas of knowledge. "Whether inside or outside school, there is reasonable agreement on the need to teach and learn mathematics, given that it is recognized that mathematical notions underlie a large part of the activities carried out in life" (SANTOS, 2008b, p.27). The reason for this understanding consists of the notion that mathematical knowledge is indispensable for people's lives and for the organization of society:

> Since mathematics is a human construction as a result of man's relationship with nature and life in society, the meaning of what is learned at school is given to the extent that the mathematical knowledge acquired by the subjects is used to understand different aspects of the culture to which they belong, to communicate and to deal with everyday situations. Measuring, counting, locating and being located, reading and interpreting information from graphs, maps and texts, arguing or counter- arguing, solving problems and communicating reasoning and results are some of the many uses of mathematics (SANTOS, 2008b, p.35).

We can say here that a mathematical education should stimulate creativity, motivating students to solve problems out of curiosity based on a proposal for meaningful learning, as well as contributing to the democratization of society, helping to foster the essential conditions for exercising citizenship and improving society.

Based on these reflections, we turned our attention to the possible contributions of mathematics teaching to education for racial relations. In this regard, Azevedo-Neto (2009, p.14) found that "the National Curriculum Parameters (PCN's) emphasize the integration of the History of Mathematics and the teaching of Mathematics with the theme of cultural plurality". This shows that the teaching of mathematics, unlike what is commonly practiced in schools, does not have an end in itself.

Investigative and pedagogical attitudes in these sociocultural perspectives, with regard to the implications of mathematics teaching for social and cultural relations, can provide a new perception and a new look at mathematics teaching, helping to overcome the contradiction between the real objectives of mathematics education and traditional forms of teaching. Costa & Oliveira (2010, p.01-02) report that:

> There are recurrent discourses that mathematics teaching should be geared towards a better understanding of reality, social phenomena, the development of citizenship and contributing to socio-historical transformations. However, on a daily basis, many math teachers feel that it is not their job to explore issues of fundamental importance, such as racial and/or cultural prejudices. Others claim that their (traditional) training does not enable them to make the necessary links between mathematical content and such problems. In fact, it is not uncommon for those who express the desire, but also the difficulties, of resizing their agendas in order to include reflections on cultural and racial diversity.

Some of the ways in which mathematics education can address race relations, especially with regard to black history and culture, can be related to work with ethnomathematics, Afroethnomathematics and African mathematical games.

There is no consensus among mathematics educators regarding the conceptualization of ethnomathematics, however, there is a general understanding that "the proposal to work along the lines of ethnomathematics has the primary objective of valuing the mathematics of different cultural groups" (D'AMBROSIO, 1989, p.18). According to Gerdes (1991, p. 32), "ethnomathematicians highlight and analyze the influence of sociocultural factors on the teaching, learning and development of mathematics". This concept seeks to understand how each culture produces mathematics that meets the specific demands of that society.

In this context of analysis, mathematics is a cultural product. In other words:

> [...] each culture develops its own way, styles and techniques of doing and responding to the search for explanations, understandings and learning. These are knowledge systems. All these systems use inference, quantification, comparison, classification, representation, measurement. Of course, Western mathematics is such a knowledge system, as a broad overview of its history shows us. But other cultures have also developed other systems of knowledge with the same objectives. These are other 'mathematics' using different ways of interfering, quantifying, comparing, classifying, representing and measuring. All these knowledge systems could be called ethnomathematics. They are the 'mathematics' of different natural and cultural environments, all motivated by the search for survival and transcendence (D'AMBROSIO, 1999, p. 52 apud. PASSOS, 2008, p.39).

An ethnomathematical approach to teaching seeks to break away from a conventional, Western-based mathematics teaching model, looking for new perspectives on mathematical knowledge and its relationship with subjects within societies. Afroethnomathematics derives from ethnomathematics, with a specific focus on the study of knowledge and mathematical production linked to Africans and people of African descent and their cultural relations with mathematics in different parts of the world. According to Cunha-Junior (2004. p.83) "the cultural uses that facilitate the learning and teaching of mathematics in these areas with a majority Afro-descendant population is the main concern of this area of knowledge". In relation to this approach to study, both in scientific research and in basic education in our country, this author reports that:

> Afroethnomathematics began in Brazil with the development of pedagogical practices by the Black Movement, in attempts to improve the teaching and learning of mathematics in quilombo communities and in urban areas where the majority of the population is of African descent, known as the black population. This Afro-ethnomathematics has been expanded by the study of African history and the elaboration of repertoires of mathematical evidence found in the various African cultures. This study of the history of mathematics on the African continent works with evidence of mathematical knowledge contained in African religious knowledge, popular myths, constructions, the arts, dangas, games, astronomy and mathematics itself, carried out on the African continent. What is done on the African continent is extended to the areas of the African diaspora (CUNHA-JUNIOR, 2004. p.83).

This approach presents itself as an important path towards a mathematics education focused on racial relations, contributing to a process of building up an image of respect for representations and knowledge of African and Afro-Brazilian origin. As D'ambrosio (2002, p. 09) states, "ethnomathematics is steeped in ethics, focused on recovering the cultural dignity of the human being". Games have been used repeatedly by various primary school teachers as facilitators of learning processes.

As Santos (2008a, p.09-10) reports:

> Many educators have long stressed the importance of visualizing and manipulating materials as a facilitator of learning. We could mention Claparede, Freinet, the Brazilian Malba Tahan, as well as Piagetl, Vygotsky, Bruner, among others. Each in their own way recognized that the individual's action on the object is basic to learning.

The use of manipulative and concrete materials, including games, has made a significant contribution to learning, especially in math education. In this respect, Santos also makes important contributions when he states that:

> Despite disagreements about how to use teaching materials to help make mathematical concepts a reality, there is widespread recognition of the importance of using games to develop logico-mathematical reasoning (2008a, p.10).

It is in this context that it becomes possible to use games of African origin for an education that goes beyond racial relations, through a contextualized work of these games, rescuing their historical and philosophical aspects and their importance for the societies from which they originate. Thus contributing to the teaching of black history and culture in mathematics education.

7 - RETHINKING THE ORIGIN OF PHILOSOPHY AND THINKING ABOUT THE ITS TEACHING FROM THE PERSPECTIVE OF RACE RELATIONS

Defining what philosophy is is difficult. There is no consensus among the various authors who have dealt with the subject throughout the history of philosophical thought. However, for the purposes of this text, we have tried to present it in summary form, seeking with a certain objectivity, to characterize it so that from there we can establish an understanding of the importance of Philosophy Teaching in basic education and the possible contributions of this to an education for racial relations.

Thus, we understand that philosophy is a body of studies focused on fundamental questions such as morality, existence and knowledge. According to Prado-Jr (1981, p.06), Philosophy consists of "a infinite and unruly speculation around any subject or question, at the whim of each author". Thus, we can say that there are a huge number of concepts and definitions of what philosophy is, which in turn depend on the interpretations of each author who deals with the subject.

This highlights the fact that philosophy is also knowledge "and in a certain way deals with the same objects as the sciences in general" (PRADO-JR 1981, p.09), although it does not constitute itself as a scientific field and differs from the sciences. According to Prado-Jr (1981, p.10), "The history of science shows us that its march and progression go uniformly in the direction of the elaboration of concepts, or rather, increasingly abstract and general 'conceptualization'." The author adds that philosophy "presents a more general and broader point of view, more essentially of the same nature, of the same objects with which science is concerned" (1981, p.12). Kneller contributes to this interpretation by stating that "science only studies those things which, in man, can be quantitatively measured. It is mainly through philosophy that we understand the total nature of man" (1970, p. 16). Thus, it doesn't necessarily need to empirically seek answers to the questions it raises, but it will use reason, the human capacity to think, to lead itself towards the answers.

Philosophy can help us to develop our thinking about certain issues and to construct logical arguments, thus helping to advance the criticality of those who study and practice it. These last points are already beginning to serve as a basis for understanding the importance of teaching philosophy in schools. When we take up the objectives of education set out in the Federal Constitution and in LDB 9394/96 with regard to preparation for the exercise of citizenship and when we think of these objectives from the perspective of an integral formation, it seems difficult to escape Philosophy in this process.

To these observations, Cotrim (1988, p.19) contributes by stating that the teaching of philosophy has the function of "developing a critical sense in students, which implies overcoming naïve and superficial conceptions about men, society and nature, conceptions forged by the dominant social 'ideology'". In other words, the study of philosophy can help us to think about and rethink our values, beliefs and prejudices because, as Geisler & Feinberg (1996, p.11) state, "the primary role of philosophy is moral, virtuous and ethical". Cotrim also adds that:

> To do this, it is necessary for philosophy teaching to stimulate the development of student reflection and provide them with a set of information about reflections already developed in the history of philosophical thought. The result of this process is a broadening of the student's reflective awareness, aimed at two fundamental sectors:
>
> * self-consciousness: criticism of oneself as a person and of one's individual and social role (self-criticism);
>
> * awareness of the world: understanding the natural and social world and its possibilities for change (1988, P.19).

We can see here how essential philosophy is as a school subject. When we understand education as a process of human, integral formation and for the exercise of citizenship, in order to provide the redefinition of values that lead us to mutual respect, equality, solidarity and social justice. Thus, Dantas (2002, p. 61) informs us that:

> Philosophy is not just another subject to be taught and learned, but it defines, practices and puts into play the essence and very nature of teaching and learning - at least insofar as we understand the nature of the educational

> process and the practice of teaching and learning, as Paulo Freire understood it, not as a simple transfer of content, or the mere acquisition of specific skills, be they technical, behavioral or cognitive, but in fact as a whole practice, a whole essentially emancipatory process of education, of forming men and women who are effectively capable of thinking, questioning and dialogically elucidating the conditions for realizing their lives, their own history, the very world in which they exist.

Based on these assumptions, we now begin to reflect on the teaching of philosophy and its possible links and contributions to an education focused on racial relations. Where an education that addresses this issue aims to contribute to the realization of democracy, seeking the inclusion and problematization of issues relating to social groups that have historically been marginalized, segregated and made invisible in society and in formal education.

To better understand these relationships, it's important to remember that the concept of democracy, the perception of the role of education in the process of democratization and integral formation, has its roots in the classical philosophy of Ancient Greece. Gadotti (1999, p.30) states that:

> Greece achieved the most advanced ideal of education in antiquity: the *paideia,* an integral education, which consisted of integrating the culture of society and the individual creation of another culture in a reciprocal influence. (...) The Greeks achieved the synthesis between education and culture: they gave enormous value to art, literature, science and philosophy. *The education of the whole man* consisted of training the body through gymnastics, the mind through philosophy and the sciences, and morals and feelings through music and the arts.

We can't neglect African philosophy itself here, because, according to Asante (2014, p.120), "philosophy began 2,800 years BC with black-skinned people from the Nile Valley, that is, 2,200 years before the appearance of Thales of Miletus, considered the first Western philosopher". The author adds that:

> [...] the practice of philosophy existed long before the Greeks. Imhotep, Ptahhotep, Amenemhat, Merikare, Duauf, Amenhotep, son of Hapu, Akhenaton and the sage of Khunanup, are just some of the African philosophers who lived long before Greece or any Greek philosopher existed (2014, p.118).

We must also take into account the fact that the word philosophy has its origins on the black continent. For, according to Asante (2014, p.118):

> There are two parts to the word "philosophy", as it has come down to us

> from the Greek, "Philo", which means friend (brother) or lover and "Sophia", which means wisdom or wise. The origin of "Sophia" is evident in the African language Mdu Ntr, the language of ancient Egypt, where the word "Seba", meaning "the wise one", appears for the first time in 2052 BC, in the tomb of Antef I, long before the existence of Graeco-Greek. The word became "Sebo" in Coptic and "Sophia" in Greek.

The author also reinforces the notes on the origin and practice of philosophy in Africa, reporting that:

> Diodorus of Sicily, a Greek writer, in his On Egypt - written in the first century before Christ - says that many of those who are "celebrated among the Greeks for their intelligence and learning, ventured to Egypt in ancient times, so that they could participate in its traditions and copy its teachings. The priests of ancient Egypt report in their history, from the records of the sacred books, that they were visited by Orpheus and Museum, Melampo, Dedalus, and, in addition to these, the poet Homer, the Spartan Lycurgus, the Athenian Solon, Plato, the philosopher Pythagoras of Samos, and the mathematician Eudoxus, as well as Democritus of Abdera and Enopides of Chios, were also there." (Asante, 2014, p.118)

These surveys show us the importance of recognizing Africanness, both for the history of philosophy and for the philosophy we have today, as well as its application in the educational field.

The educational process, as far as philosophy teaching is concerned, cannot be disassociated from the social and cultural contexts experienced by its subjects. Racial and cultural diversity make up these contexts. Based on this observation, and by working with the issue of race, it is important to create the conditions for students to question, think about and rethink concepts and values that relate to the history and cultures of black origin, using a philosophical dimension for the reflections that will be made. Ribeiro (2012, p.196) contributes to this reflection by pointing out that:

> A new epistemology is possible based on the cultural experience of the black people and a new axiology, a new theory of value based on a philosophy of life and knowledge, of writings and expressions that spring from the historical experience of the Afro-Brazilian people who express the "beauty" of their life, their art and their elaborations.

With this, through philosophy, we can reflect on the racial relations that exist in our society, with issues related to racism, racial inequalities, the myth of racial democracy, acculturation and religious intolerance. These are the paths towards a transformative education, where respect and dialogue with others can be established.

8 - INTERDISCIPLINARITY: A POSSIBLE PATH FOR RACIAL RELATIONS EDUCATION

The meaning of being at school goes beyond learning specific codes and content to meet certain objectives linked to external issues such as entrance exams or the interests of the job market. Attending school means the opportunity to access forms of learning so that one can read and interpret the world in its multiple dimensions and complexity. Cartesianism, which was of fundamental importance to the development of the sciences since the Enlightenment in the 18th century, gave them a body and specificities, a characteristic that also permeated the organization of school knowledge. As Santos (1995) puts it, "Cartesianism (Descartes 1596-1650) went on to organize the entire social and educational system and shaped the WAY MEN THINK for the last 400 years".

As a result, we have a school that is organized in a disciplinary way, through its modules that fragment knowledge, establishing little or no connection between the knowledge of the different areas that make up school subjects. According to Castanho (1989, p. 21), this segmented way of organizing knowledge:

> a compartmentalized view of reality is produced, there is no interaction between the parts, one is disconnected from the other. Underlying this way of seeing society in a fragmented way, this phenomenon of emasculating the ability to think in terms of structures, is the accumulative conception of knowledge, the conception that learning means absorbing information and not analyzing it or relating it to one another.

The contradiction there appears because knowledge of the world, of everyday experiences, is not presented to us in a fragmented way outside of school, reality is not disciplinary. However, the sciences take them for themselves as objects of investigation, casting their gaze over the parts of the whole and giving their explanations. Kneller (1970, p. 12) reports that:

> A major defect of many specialists and also of many students is the tendency to consider special studies as supreme importance, due to the fact that we live in an age of specialization. Putting aside the provinciality of such an attitude, the fact remains that we cannot properly deal with any single subject until we have a working knowledge of what it means to exist, to

know, to evaluate and to inquire about things in general.

The various phenomena, whether physical (natural) or anthropic, have different dimensions and a comprehensive understanding of them requires a reading that involves knowledge of various sciences. Let's take the example of a landslide in a hillside area, or the collapse of a dam that results in the displacement of a large volume of sediment, water or tailings over urban and rural areas. We would need to draw on the knowledge of different areas such as Climatology, Geology, History, Geography, Sociology, Anthropology, Mathematics, Physics, Agronomy, Engineering, Economics, Politics, Law, Chemistry, Biology and so on. so that we can give reasonable explanations of the causes and effects of these phenomena. How could sociology, history and geography explain certain phenomena in the course of historical processes without the help of statistical data, which in turn depends on mathematics to be produced? What conditions certain urban engineering works if not the very social and urban dynamics of the society for which they are intended? How can we manage the production of food, which drives a territory's economy and supplies its people, without paying attention to its climatic characteristics, soils, relief and potential for distribution and consumption? How can we think of a nation's progress taking into account only the economic growth promoted by the different sectors of the economy, neglecting social development?

How can we understand social problems such as racial issues without taking into account historical, geographical, economic, social, cultural and territorial processes? According to Morin (2002, p. 36), "knowledge of information or data in isolation is insufficient. It is necessary to place information and data in their context so that they acquire meaning". In other words, in order to understand the whole, there needs to be a dialogue between the parts (the sciences), something that is perfectly possible.

It is possible, much more than that, it is desirable and interdisciplinarity represents one possibility along this path.

Interdisciplinarity consists of the correlation between two or more disciplines when approaching a common theme. To this end, the PCN stresses that

> It is important to emphasize that interdisciplinarity presupposes an integrating axis, which can be the object of knowledge, a research project or an intervention plan. In this sense, it must start from the need felt by schools, teachers and students to explain, understand, intervene, change, predict, something that challenges an isolated discipline and attracts the attention of more than one eye, perhaps several. (BRASIL, 2000, p.76).

Interdisciplinarity is an essential condition for contextualized teaching that is capable of reconnecting knowledge and thus providing students with the development of a critical reading of the world, but its practice is constituted as attitudes that "depend on culture, the communication of specialists and transcending their own specialty, becoming aware of their own limits in order to welcome the contributions of other disciplines" (FRANCISCHETT, 2005, p.01). Thus, for Japiassu:

> [...] the true interdisciplinary spirit consists of that attitude of epistemological vigilance capable of leading each specialist to open up to other specialties different from his own, to be attentive to everything in the other disciplines that could enrich his field of research (1976, p.138).

This attitude can thus create the conditions for the development of meaningful learning, through the attribution of meaning to the contents and curricular components for the learner.

According to article 210 of the Brazilian Federal Constitution of 1988, "minimum content will be set for primary education, in order to ensure a common basic education and respect for national and regional cultural and artistic values".

In order to meet this constitutional requirement and social demand, the National Curriculum Parameters - PCN - were published in 1997 by the Ministry of Education - MEC. This proposal brought with it the inclusion of cross-cutting themes, which address issues related to ethics, cultural plurality, environment, health, sexual orientation and local issues, given the possibilities for discussion and formative work on the themes selected. As the document (PCN) states, "the inclusion of cross-cutting themes requires taking a stance on fundamental and urgent problems in social life".

Affirming the indispensability of an education that takes cultural diversity into account, the PCNs present Cultural Plurality as a cross-cutting theme and the perspectives in which it should be worked on:

> The theme of Cultural Plurality concerns knowledge and appreciation of the ethnic and cultural characteristics of the different social groups that live together in the national territory, socio-economic inequalities and criticism of the discriminatory and exclusionary social relations that permeate Brazilian society, offering students the chance to get to know Brazil as a complex, multifaceted and sometimes paradoxical country (p.121).

Here we are referring to contents linked to cultural plurality, which are those related to racial diversity, which in turn needs to be worked on in basic education, not only because of the legal prescription dealt with in Law 10.639/03, but because of the importance of this approach for the establishment of a truly democratic education. As Gomes (2001) reports:

> Thinking about the link between education, citizenship and race means going beyond discussions about cross-cutting themes or emerging curricular proposals. It represents a questioning of the centrality of the racial issue in our pedagogical practice, in educational projects and policies and in the struggle for a democratic society that guarantees the right to citizenship for all (p.83-84).

It is up to the schools and their professionals to recognize their commitment to the exercise of this education, understanding the spaces that each of the disciplines can occupy in this process, always seeking communication and interrelationship between these various school disciplines in the organization of pedagogical work in order to contemplate the practice of education for racial relations and anti-racism. And with regard to interdisciplinarity, understanding that the racial issue has significant potential for establishing links between school knowledge.

Thinking of interdisciplinarity as a way of educating about racial relations, through dialogue between school subjects, we will present some reflections on other subjects and their knowledge, in search of their possible relationship with racial issues. We hope that these analyses will help to develop strategies for interdisciplinary work involving the teaching of History and Geography and other school knowledge.

FINAL CONSIDERATIONS

A starting point for reflection on the importance and possible contributions of material like this to the work of primary school teachers is the following question: what should the teacher's attitude be towards education on race relations? Thus, we believe that in order to carry out an education for racial relations from the perspective of Law 10.639/03, it is important for teachers to act and play a leading role, promoting discussions and reflections in the school environment on issues related to racism and anti-racism in society and education and that value interdisciplinary practices in the students' formative processes.

In this way, we hope that this theoretical material can help teachers to construct work proposals that make it possible to seek an integration between teachers and school knowledge in the processes of discussing themes linked to racial issues in education.

In order to do this, it is necessary for teachers to engage in dialogue and reflect on issues related to racism, anti-racism and racial inequalities in Brazil; to analyze the role of Law 10. 639/03 in the context of affirmative action policies; and, within the specifics of this proposal, to identify the role of History and Geography teaching in the context of education for racial relations.639/03 in the context of affirmative action policies; within the specificity of this proposal, to identify the role of History and Geography teaching in the context of education for racial relations, seeking an interdisciplinary approach with other school subjects; and, above all, to transform this knowledge into educational practices.

The aim of this material is to help teachers reflect on this issue, creating the conditions for them to devise and develop pedagogical strategies to address racial issues, using interdisciplinary practices as a way forward. Contributing to the promotion of an anti-racist education that respects and values black history and culture.

The discussions aim to stimulate teachers' investigative curiosity about the subject and their area of training and work in basic education, leading them to think and rethink their pedagogical practices, in order to seek a direction that is geared towards education for racial relations, anti-racism and the valorization of black history and culture and the adoption of an interdisciplinary stance in their approaches.

We know that this material is a "brick" in the construction of this education. But we know that the more racial issues become part of educational thinking, teacher training and pedagogical practices, the closer we will be to seeing this "work" completed.

REFERENCES

ALENCAR, Claudiana Nogueira de. et al. Peasant identity and representation: for a critical analysis of literary discourse. In: PINHEIRO, Helder et al (org). **Literature and the formation of readers**. Campina Grande: Bagagem, 2008. p. 127-142.

ASANTE, Molefi Kete, An African origin of philosophy: Myth or reality. **Journal of Humanities and Letters**, v. 1, n. 1, 2014.

AZEVEDO-NETO, Leonardo Dourado de. Law no. 10.639: how can the inclusion of knowledge from African roots be achieved in mathematics teaching? In: **V Seminario Racismo & Educagao e IV Seminario de Genero, Raga e Etnia**, 2009, Uberlandia. 2009. p. 13-20.

BARBOSA, Ana Mae. **Topicos, utopicos**. Belo Horizonte: C / Arte, 1998.

Inquietagoes e Mudangas no Ensino da Arte. Sao Paulo: Cortez, 2003.

BARBOSA, Ana Mae. **Contemporary art education: Consonances international**. 2ª ed. Sao Paulo; Cortez, 2008.

BRAZIL. Constitution (1988). **Constitution of the Federative Republic of Brazil**. Brasilia, DF: Senado Federal: Centro Grafico, 1988.

BRASIL. **Parametros Curriculares Nacionais: Apresentagao dos temas transversais**. Brasilia: MEC/SEF, v. 8, p. 146, 1997.

BRAZIL. **National Curriculum Parameters: Art**. Brasilia: MEC/SEF, 1997.

BRASIL. **Parametros curriculares nacionais: Ciencias Naturais**. Brasilia: MEC/SEF, 1997.

BRASIL. Parametros **Curriculares Nacionais: Introduto aos Parametros Curriculares Nacionais Parametros Curriculares Nacionais**: MEC/SEF, 1997.

BRAZIL. **National Curriculum Parameters: Cultural Plurality**. Brasilia: MEC/SEF, v. 10.2. MEC/SEF, 1997.

BRAZIL. Law No. 10.639, of January 9, 2003. Amends Law No. 9.394, of December 20, 1996, which establishes the guidelines and bases of national education, to include the theme "Afro-Brazilian History and Culture" in the official school curriculum, and makes other provisions. **Diario Oficial da Uniao**. Brasilia, DF, January 9, 2003.

BRASIL. **Parametros Curriculares Nacionais: Ensino Medio**. Brasilia: MEC, 2000.

BRASIL. **Parecer CNE/CP n.° 3, de 10 de margo de 2004**. Brasilia: MEC, 2004.

BRASIL. **Resolugao CNE/CP. n° 1, de 17 de junho de 2004**. Brasilia: MEC, 2004.

CALLAI, Helena Copetti. **The formation of the geography professional: the teacher**. Ijui: Unijui, 2013.

CASTANHO, M. E. L. M. A didatica no ensino da filosofia no 2° grau. **Revista Reflexao**, n. 43, 1989.

CASTELLANI-FILHO, Lino. **Polftica educacional e educagao ffsica**. (Polemicas do Nosso Tempo) Campinas, SP: Autores Associados, 1998.

CIRQUEIRA, Diogo Margal; CORREA, Gabriel Siqueira. The ethno-racial question in Brazilian geography: An introductory debate on academic production in postgraduate courses. In: **XII Coloquio Internacional de Geocrftica**, 2012, Bogota - Colombia. XII Colloquio Internacional de Geocrftica. Bogota: Universidad Nacional de Colombia, 2012. v. 1. p. 1-14.

FEDERAL COUNCIL FOR PHYSICAL EDUCATION. School physical education. **Revista Educagao Ffsica**. NO. 05 - DECEMBER 2002.

COSTA, Wanderleya Nara Gongalves; OLIVEIRA, Cristiane Coppe. Mathematics education and racial prejudice: African and Afro-Brazilian cultures in the classroom. In: Proceedings **of the X National Meeting of Mathematics Education**. Salvador: SBEM, 2010

COTRIM, Gilberto. **Fundamentals of Philosophy for a Conscious Generation** . Sao Paulo: Ed. Saraiva, 1988 - 3ª edition.

CUNHA-JUNIOR, Henrique. Afroethnomathematics, Africa and Afro-descendancy. **Themes in Education**, v. 13, p. 83-95, 2004.

D'AMBROSIO, Beatriz S. How to teach mathematics today. **Temas e debates**, v. 2, n. 2, p. 15-19, 1989.

D'AMBROSIO, Ubiratan. **Ethnomathematics - the link between tradition and modernity**. Belo Horizonte: Autentica, 2002.

DAMIANI, Amelia Luisa. Geography and the construction of citizenship. In: **Geography in the classroom**. Sao Paulo: Contexto, p. 50-61, 1999.

DANTAS, R. Philosophy, education and history. In: KOHAN, W. (Org.). **Teaching philosophy: perspectives**. Belo Horizonte: Autentica, 2002.

D'AVILA, Jerry. **Diploma of whiteness: social and racial policy in Brazil:** 19171945. Translated by Claudia Santana Martins. Sao Paulo: UNESP, 2006.

DIWAN, Pietra. **Raga Pura: a history of eugenics in Brazil and the world**. Sao Paulo: Contexto, 2007.

ESPINHEIRA-FILHO, Ivan de Pinho. **"Eu sou negao, meu coragao e a liberdade": dialog about black or Afro-Brazilian literature in high schools in Bahia**. Dissertation (Master's in Education) - Faculty of Education - Federal University of Bahia - Salvador, 2013.

FELIPE, Delton Aparecido; TERUYA, Teresa Kazuko. TEACHING AFRICAN HISTORY AND CULTURE IN BRAZILIAN CLASSROOMS. **Proceedings of the**

PPE Research Seminar. Maringa State University - Postgraduate Program in Education, 2010.

FERNANDES, Jose Ricardo Oria. History teaching and cultural diversity: challenges and possibilities. **Cadernos Cedes**, v. 25, n. 67, p. 378-388, 2005.

FIGUEIREDO. Lenita Miranda. **Art History for children**. Sao Paulo: Pioneira, 1991.

FONSECA, Maria Nazareth Soares. Literatura negra, literatura afro-brasileira: como responder a polemica? (in) SOUZA, Forentina; LIMA, Nazare (org.). **Literatura afro-brasileira**. Salvador: Center for Afro-Oriental Studies; Brasilia: Palmares Cultural Foundation, 2006.

FRANCISCHETT, Mafalda Nesi. Understanding interdisciplinarity in everyday life. **Colloquium promoted by the Master's Program in Letters at UNIOESTE-Cascavel**. Cascavel, 2005.

GADOTTI, Moacir. **History of Pedagogical Ideas**. Sao Paulo; Atica, 1999.

GEISLER, Norman L.; FEINBERG, Paul D. **Introduction to philosophy: a Christian perspective**. Translated by Gordon Chown. 2ª ed., Sao Paulo: Vida Nova, 1996.

GERDES, Paulus. **Ethnomathematics: culture, mathematics, education**. Mogambique: ISP, 1991.

GOMES, Nilma Lino. Citizen education, ethnicity and race: the pedagogical treatment of diversity. In: **Racism and anti-racism in education: rethinking our school**. Sao Paulo: Selo Negro, p. 83-96, 2001.

GUIMARAES, Antonio Sergio Alfredo. How to work with "raga" in sociology. **Educagao e Pesquisa**, v. 29, n. 1, p. 93-107, 2003.

HERNANDEZ, Fernando. **Visual Culture, Educational Change and Work Projects**. Translated by: Jussara Haubert Rodrigues. Porto Alegre: Artes Medicas, 2000. p. 261.

JAPIASSU, Hilton. **Interdisciplinarity and the Pathology of Knowledge**. Riode Janeiro: Imago, 1976.

JENKINS, Keith. **History rethought**. Sao Paulo: Contexto, 2005.

KNELLER, George F. **Introdugao a Filosofia da Educagao**. Rio de Janeiro: Zahar Editores, 1970.

LARROSA, Jorge. Literature, experience and formation: an interview by Jorge Larrosa with Alfredo Veiga-Neto. In: COSTA, M. V. (org.). **Caminhos investigativos: novos olhares na pesquisa em educagao**. Porto Alegre: Mediagao, 1996.

LIMA, Monica. Making the drums sound: teaching the history of Africa and Africans in Brazil. In: **Cadernos Pedagogicos PENESB**, n. 5, p. 159-171. Niteroi: Editora da UFF, 2004.

MATTOS, Ivanilde Guedes. **The negation of the black body: representations of the body in physical education teaching**. 2007. Dissertation (Master's in Education) - Department of Education Campus I - Bahia State University, Salvador, 2007.

MIGUEL, Jose Carlos. Teaching mathematics from the perspective of concept formation: theoretical and methodological implications. Nucleos de Ensino: **Articles from Projects carried out in 2003**, p. 375-394, 2005.

MOREIRA, Analia de Jesus; SILVA, Maria Cecilia de Paula; DOMINGUES, Soraya Correia. Law n° 10.639/03 and the teaching of physical education: didactic-methodological possibilities for ethno-racial education. (annals) **Congres international de L'afirse - V e colloque national afirse-section brasilienne. Educational policies and practices**. 18-21 octobre 2009.

MORIN, Edgar. **The seven knowledges necessary for the education of the future**. Sao Paulo: Cortez; Brasilia: Unesco, 2002.

MORRISH, Ivor. **Sociology of education: an introduction**. Translation by Alvaro Cabral, technical revision by Jether Pereira Ramalho. 2ª ed. Rio de Janeiro, Zabar; Brasilia, INL, 1975.

OLIVA, Anderson Ribeiro. The History of Africa on school benches. Representations and inaccuracies in didactic literature. **Estudos afro-asiaticos**, v. 25, n. 3, p. 421-461, 2003.

OLIVEIRA, Luiz Fernandes de. Anti-racist education: tensions and challenges for sociology teaching. **Educagao & Realidade**, v. 39, n. 1, p. 81-98, 2014.

OLIVEIRA, Vitor Marinho. **What is physical education?** (First Steps), Sao Paulo: Brasiliense, 2004.

PARANA, **Basic Education Curriculum Guidelines**. Curitiba: SEED, p. 57, 2008.

PASSOS, Caroline Mendes dos. **Ethnomathematics and critical mathematics education: theoretical and practical connections**. 2008. 150f. 2008. Dissertation (Master's in Education) - Faculty of Education - Federal University of Minas Gerais, Belo Horizonte.

PORTO-GONQALVES, Carlos Walter. The geography of the social: a contribution to the methodological debate on the study of conflicts and social movements in Latin America. **Revista Eletronica AGB-TL**, v. 1, n. 3, p. 5-26, 2006.

PRADO-JR, Caio. **What is Philosophy**? Sao Paulo: Editora Brasiliense, 1981.

RATTS, Alecsandro Jose Prudencio. Ethnicities and others: the spatialities of encounters/confrontations. In: **Revista Espago e Cultura**. Rio de Janeiro, NEPEC/UERJ, N° 17-18, p. 77-89, 2004.

RIBEIRO, Obertal Xavier. Axiology: philosophy and ethno-racial relations, the construction of values in educational practices. **identidade!**, v. 17, n. 2, p. 189-204, 2012.

SANTOS, Akiko. **What is transdisciplinarity**? Rural Semanal, n. 31/32, 1995.

SANTOS, Celso Jose dos. **African games and mathematics education: sowing seeds with the Mancala family**. Maringa: State Department of Education-UEM, 2008a.

SANTOS, Lorene dos. Teaching History and Law 10.639/03: dialogues between fields of knowledge, curriculum guidelines and the challenges of practice-DOI: 10.5752/P. 2237-8871.2011 v12n17p59. **Cadernos de Historia**, v. 12, n. 17, p. 59-92, 2012.

SANTOS, Renato Emerson dos. Geography teaching and the curriculum: issues based on Law 10.639. **Terra Livre**, v. 1, n. 34, p.141-160, 2010.

SANTOS, Renato Emerson dos. Law 10.639 and Geography Teaching: Building a research-action agenda. In: **Tamoios Magazine**. Year VII. N° 1, 2011.

SANTOS, Vinicio de Macedo et al. School mathematics, the student and the teacher: apparent paradoxes and polarizations under discussion. **Cad. CEDES**, Campinas, v. 28, n. 74, 2008b.

SANTOS, Wellington Oliveira dos. Law 10.639/03 and geography textbooks. **POIESIS Magazine**. Unisul, Tubarao, v.8, n.13, p. 229 - 247, Jan/Jun 2014.

SILVA, Maria Jose Lopes da. The arts and ethno-cultural diversity in primary school. In. MUNANGA, Kabengele (org.). **Overcoming racism at school**. [Brasilia]: Ministry of Education, Department of Continuing Education,
Literacy and Diversity, 2008

SILVA, Douglas Verrangia Correa da. **Ethnic-racial relations education in science teaching: possible dialogues between Brazil and the United States**. 335p. Thesis (Doctorate in Education) - Center for Education and Human Sciences - Federal University of Sao Carlos - Sao Carlos - SP, 2009.

SILVA, Maria Rodrigues da. Afro-Brazilian children's literature. **Cadernos Imbondeiro**. Joao Pessoa, v.1, n.1, 2010.

SOUZA, Florentina; LIMA Nazare (Orgs.). **Afro-Brazilian Literature**. Salvador: Center for Afro-Oriental Studies; Brasilia: Palmares Cultural Foundation, 2006. 220p.

TONINI, Ivaine Maria. Ethnic scenes in geography textbooks. **Proceedings of the 1st Brazilian Congress on the History of Education**. Rio de Janeiro, 2000.

VAZZOLER, Leomar dos Santos. **The racial question in Geography teaching**. Dissertation (Master's in Education) - Center for Applied Social Studies - Fluminense Federal University, Niteroi, 2006.

VERRANGIA, Douglas. The training of science and biology teachers and traditional knowledge of African and Afro-Brazilian origin. Magis. **Magazine International Research in Education**, v. 6, n. 12, p. 105-117, 2013.

VYGOTSKY, L. S. **The social formation of the mind: the development of higher psychological processes**. 6 ed. Sao Paulo: Martins Fontes, 1998.

WERTHEIN, Jorge. Introduction. In: SILVA-JR, Hedio. **Racial Discrimination in Schools: between the law and social practices**. Brasilia: UNESCO, 2002.

Printed by Books on Demand GmbH, Norderstedt / Germany